Pieces From

A Beating Heart

Rashad Solo

(@R.Solo)

Cover By: Olu Adedugbe
(@oludamo)

Illustrations By: Andre Barnwell
(@sex.n.sandwiches)

Contents

Love

Loss

Life After

To the Queen that did her best and beyond to raise a King,

My Mother

Pieces From A Beating Heart

"First Impression"

There was no marginalizing her
She was limitless
Free to do as she pleased
The world was her oyster
She was its pearl
The sands of time
Had no effect
On her effulgence
Beauty emanated from her soul
Not skin
She was timeless classic
Like that line from a movie
You'll never forget
Memorable
First kiss
Unforgettable
First time
Divine
Like being baptized
I mean...
She was the type
Of woman you prayed for
Thank God.

Pieces From A Beating Heart

"Showers"

Maybe it's the rain
That has me feeling this way
But I can't shake it
As the raindrops hit
I think about my lips
Against your skin
And how my lightning
Strikes between
Your thighs
As you thunder
For more
Category 5
Such a Beautiful Storm

"The Rush"

He flew out of the driveway like a bat out of hell, almost wiping out the mailbox to their home. The engine of his car roared, disturbing the quiet, suburban streets of their neighborhood. He was fuming upset, though he couldn't quite recall how the argument started. He knew too well how it ended...Ugly.

It wasn't the first time they fought, but their fights seemed to get progressively worse. The words cut deeper and he was quicker to leave. Maybe he became more impatient...Maybe she became more agitated. Either way, the arguments were draining and taking a toll on their relationship.

He pulled over a couple of blocks from their home to collect his thoughts. He didn't want to leave, but he was tired of fighting. It seemed like every night, a new problem would arise that could only be resolved with shouting and name calling. It was exhausting, but he had to take responsibility for his faults when they argued.

He shouted when she screamed. He cursed at her just as vigorously as she called him every form of filth. But when her words cut too deep and he had nothing as witty to say, he would be quick to leave before the situation escalated any further. He wanted her to wonder if he would return, but he often ended up wondering why he ever left. What did they fight about? Dirty dishes, lifted toilet seats, eyelashes in the sink...Comfortable shit that could be overlooked. Instead, they nitpicked over trivial details to get under each other's skin. The infractions were never serious enough to warrant their dramatic reactions. Petty things shouldn't come between their love.

He weighed the pros and cons as he sat in his car. The scales were heavily in her favor. She was everything he wanted and her attitude was probably what he needed, even if he couldn't see it. He just knew she was not the one to lose.

The bat flew back to the cave with the same hellish speed from where it came, almost swiping the mailbox again in the same way. It didn't matter how the fight started. He would end it.

Pieces From A Beating Heart

She had opened the door of their house when she heard his car and stood in its frame with her arms crossed. She began addressing him as he exited the car and began his walk across the grass towards her.

"You always want to just run away when I'm trying talk to you," she began as he came closer towards her. "You don't ever want to listen and always want to catch an attitude when things aren't going your way. You're not a baby. With these damn tantrums! And now you think you're just going to stroll back in here like everything is ok? No way!"

She shook her head as he stopped in front of her, rolling her eyes in anticipation of his lame excuse...No excuse came.

"Shut up," he responded softly as her jaw dropped.

She stood there shocked, but the moment was short lived. Before she could become livid, they were kissing and she was lifted into the air.

Pieces From A Beating Heart

Against the open door, he tore at her clothes and she didn't care. She just wanted him to be happy with her, she always wanted him near. The fights were just spice to their life because deep down, they both knew...

The love wasn't going anywhere.

"Appraisal"

She inspires art
Because she is a work of it
I paint for her
The words foreplay
Making her brain wet
As she lets go
Of inhibitions
We act off
Of instinct
Movements in sync
She tastes like pink
Starburst
She is a work of art
With the heart
Of a king
This queen
Is a masterpiece
I aim to please
For I am the painter
And she is the canvas
It pleases me
To hit these strokes
Have her sing along

Pieces From A Beating Heart

To these keys
As I ensure she
Hits all the right notes
As we perfect
Harmony.

"Nova"

A Solar Eclipse
A Blood Hued Moon
You're Once In A Lifetime
If Even That Lucky
Which Is Why
I Thank The Stars
That You Are
Part Of My Universe.

"The Menu Part One"

I got caught up in her physical, so much so it felt spiritual. Like something inside of me had been awakened for the first time by the look in her eyes. She noticed my stare and addressed my attraction head on.

"This is not eye candy. I'm more like soul food."

I wondered if she knew how my heart hungered for something deeper. I envisioned myself devouring the delicacies that were her thoughts, ingesting the nutriments derived from her knowledge, all while dining on her intellect as she seduced me with her sultry intelligence. Magnificent, heaven sent it seemed. No crown gleamed on her head, but evidently, I was in the presence of a Queen.

Humbly, I pursued a proper course of action to react to her up front nature. I had never been a player, games were not my thing. By the looks of her, I knew men often played with her emotions, hoping to have a night with her...But she knew her worth. She wasn't a one night stand, no man's side situation, or a fuck friend. She didn't judge others for their standards, just knew they didn't add up to how she wanted to live.

 Their plots to sleep with her only worked in hardening her heart against the next man to try. I didn't shy away from the challenge or pretend like she was not the woman I came for. I had to express my genuine intentions without coming off aggressive.

"I know that there's depth behind the beauty I see. That you have more to offer than what meets the eye and I'm inclined to find out what's on your mind. So before we decide to try to figure out our compatibility physically, can you and I try to connect mentally?"

She couldn't decline my offer...

"Effort"

She was worth working for
So I worked harder than any man that came
Before me so she would know
How valuable her love was
I had dealt with so much
To be able to trust her
Was a comfort I couldn't take for granted
Loyalty was a gift and I appreciated
What she had to give
I wasn't going to be a good man to her
I would be a King.

"Waiting Game"

How long am I supposed to wait until I can say I
love you?
What if I felt it on the first date, but didn't want
you to look at me crazy? Is it possible that, at first
sight, in a world with billions of people, that I
could identify you as the one for me? Can it be?
Can I find trust and love in a generation that only
wants to fuck? When popular belief is that having
feelings is a weakness so we should cover them
up? You show me the real you, not who you think
I want you to be. You bear your flaws and your
heart courageously, making me wonder...
How long am I supposed to wait until I can say I
love you?

"Apothecary"

Your Presence
Is the Pleasure
That Takes Away
The Pain.

"Ultimatum"

He stopped calling as much. The texts were less frequent, his reason being work, but she took it as an excuse. It wasn't settling her nerves because she had heard it before. She saw less of him and when they did spend time, he spent most of it sleeping versus acknowledging her presence. She was convinced that something was wrong.

She couldn't place her finger on it and started snooping. She decided to check his phone, but saw no conversations that implied he was cheating. She even looked at what he said to his boys, knowing he would confide truths to them that he may not share with her, but she still had no clue as to what he was up to. Not knowing was killing her.

Her insecurities were killing him. Things had changed, but not in the way she suspected. He didn't neglect her for other women or try to sneak off to do his own things. He wasn't tired from cheating, but physically drained from exhausting days where he worked hard to provide better. For them.

Enough was enough. He had heard enough of her complaints. Nothing short of confrontation would get her to see. The next time she addressed him with her wild accusations, he didn't hesitate on giving her a piece of his mind.

"Shut up," he began, "Just shut up for a minute. I love you and nothing has changed. I understand, you may have dealt with boys that told you the same. You had boyfriends before me that adored you and found comfort in other women all the same...
But I'm not them. This is not a game. I'm with you because I see qualities that make me want to wife you, I'm not here to waste your time. So baby...Please stop. If you can't trust me and my love for you? By all means, leave."

She stood there, shocked and aroused by the sound of his voice. He had never spoken to her like that before and the confidence in his tone drove his point home. Why should she stress what she didn't know and couldn't prove? Why lose a good man over her history with fools? Especially when this good man proved his worth

and showed nothing less. Her apology ensued
and the issue was lost between the sheets.

They loved happily ever after.

"Uphill"

She built barriers
To protect her heart
He scaled walls
To show her
How much she deserved
To be loved.

"Solo Cents"

We go through shit
Key word being We.

The best things in life don't come easy. They are worth fighting for. Relationships aren't always going to be a breeze, but the best ones can persist through the storm. So hold on to one another. Remember, love is strong enough to overcome anything...You just need to believe.

"Universal"

I was mystified
By her eyes
A beautiful hue
But their shade
Was not what
Captured me

Initially
I was baffled
By the feeling
Seeing her gave
And wanted to
Unravel her mystery
I had to get
A closer look

I took steps towards her
As curiosity conquered
My usual trepidations
Of public places
I stopped once
I obtained a better view
No longer confused

Pieces From A Beating Heart

As to why I was
So drawn
To her eyes

Her stare was more than
Seeing stars in the sky
She was worth galaxies
Like a universe in disguise
I mean...

It was mind blowing
How her soul flowed
From those eyes
I knew at that moment
I would trade the world
For her
To Be
Mine.

"Scene"

We had date nights, when we decided to get out of the house and take a night on the town. Simple nights, where we decided to spend time enjoying each other's company in the public eye versus being cuddled up inside. I never complained either way, but I did enjoy showing you off to the world.

I was proud to be your man, elated that you were with me, and unafraid to show how much I appreciated your love. This night was nothing special. Just dinner and a movie, but the way you were moving? I was losing my mind.

"You're so fine."

That's all I thought as I watched you get dressed. From the application of your make up, to the way you did your hair, I couldn't help but stare. Your matching bra and panties, the dress you decided to wear...All of you amazed me. I couldn't contain my admiration. We didn't make it to dinner. That night, we made a movie...On location.

Pieces From A Beating Heart

"Solo Cents"

More Than My Heart
You Are
The Reason It Beats

*Love is about vulnerability. It is about openness.
It is about giving a person the power to destroy
you and trusting that they will not. That's what
love is. So if you're not ready for that level of
commitment due to the things you've been
through, it's understandable. Love isn't for the
faint of heart.*

"Commitment"

I Won't Let
A World Full Of Lust
Affect Our Love
Trust That I'll
Fight Temptations
And Claim You As My Own
Without Hesitation
Let Me Ease Your Reservations
Put Your Heart In My Hands
And I Promise To Hold You
Until Time Ends

"Recognition"

Soul mate,
I belonged
To you
Before
I Knew
Your name.

"Mr Wayne"

I carry her bag
If she needs
I'll also beat your ass for my queen
If she needs
Her Dark Knight in shining armor
Her Allegiance
Is an Honor
Jokers can't harm us
Solid as a rock
Protected by our karma
Our love won't die
It just grows stronger.

"Unexpected"

It hit us like a whirlwind
Spinning in an oasis
Where a sip
From her ocean
Tasted like Ambrosia
Swimming in her sweetness
Peaking
Hitting a climax
That left more
Than our knees weak
It strengthened our souls
Lifted our spirits
And confirmed that
She was mine and I?
Am here
Spinning in this whirlwind
Tethered to her
To weather the storm
With love as our only guide
Leading our hearts home.

"Talk less."

I didn't expect to woo her with my words. When I told her how I would treat her, I didn't expect her to believe me. I was sure men had said everything under the sun to get her attention, but I wasn't concerned with them or her past. I took the time and put forth the effort in showing her the weight of my words. I didn't call her a Queen. I treated her like one.

"Solo Cents"

My loyalty, above all else, is hers. Potentially, she is my wife and the mother of my child...What other side would I choose? She is me for we are one and there is no separating us.

Other people shouldn't be involved in every aspect of your relationship. That doesn't mean you have to stay inside, cooped up with the person you're with. I mean this in the sense that, other people's opinions are just opinions...You're the person living in your relationship. Friends can give all the advice they want, but I'd advise you to follow your heart. You are the only one who knows what your happiness requires.

"Timeline"

Her love was so
Legendary
My moves were so
Classic
Grasping at sand
She was shaped like an
Hourglass
Eternity could pass
She'd still be the
Baddest on the planet
Satanic
I had to have
Her Forever
Never settle lifestyle
Till death
I attest
She's the best
Angelic.

"Fiend"

I'm lying in this bed alone
Wishing I was next to you
Usually I played it cool
But lately?
I've been sweating you
Even though it's the middle of winter
This feeling's like June
Passion burning bright
Fueled by thoughts of you
The lovebug bit me
Pierced my skin
And drew blood
You entered my veins
My blessed
True love.

"Pulse"

You're Extraordinarily Rare
With An Air Of Perfection
Utterly Intoxicating
Yet Subtly Refreshing
I Keep Trying To Catch My Breath
Because Your Love Is Such A Rush
But My Cardiac's Arrested

"Vow"

I'll be damned
If I ever let another man
Love you
The way I'm destined to.

"Spoken Word"

Her words were versed into lines
That sung to my soul
She was Poetry.

Flowing freely through my veins
Behind her bars of Art
Life in Her Sentence
I was lost in her system
For She was Poetry

The Stanzas
Of her Wordplay
Held me captive
Ever-lasting Love
To me
You're Poetry.

"Solo Cents"

Who knew doing nothing with someone could feel like everything?

Appreciate the smallest of gestures, like the mere presence of another person. Being with someone you love is a gift, being able to share experiences is a blessing, so don't take the moments you have together for granted. The true beauty in life is that it can be over at any time, so appreciate each moment for it truly could be your last. Smile, laugh, live...Love.

"The Menu Part 2"

Her appetite for knowledge was appealing. I couldn't reveal my thirst, but from our first words, I knew I wanted more of her. Usually, I proceeded with caution as I was often a victim of unfortunate circumstances when it came to finding romance, but I felt a familiarity with her.

It may have been the first time I saw her face, but my imagination raced with memories we hadn't even made. My heart fluttered with a feeling I couldn't place and I didn't bother trying to identify it with a name. I just ran with it...I just swam in the depths of her intellect until I grew tired and drowned out of consciousness to the sound of her voice...

Only to awake the next day and crave the same fate. She had me hooked to her energy and effortlessly invaded my reservations. My feelings were guarded, but I couldn't bare keeping her out. It felt like an obsession with how often thoughts of her crossed my mind, to the point I began questioning my own sanity...Like how was I ever alright without her?

Crazy how one person could come and change how you look at life. I had been committed to

Pieces From A Beating Heart

staying single, mingling with appetizing treats that were never given much of me. Then she came, a full course with your choice of dessert and a cup of coffee, all on the house. She was so good I doubted she was real...

But the feelings she gave me couldn't have been fake. The way we connected was majestic and we continued to flow. We continued to grow together until we became inseparable. A perfect pairing like herring and white wine until time itself wondered, could it outlast you and I? I think not...We are forever.

"Royalty"

You were all I ever wanted
When we got together
I felt nothing would come
Between us
I trusted we would
Make it through any storm
We bonded on another level

You were more than special
You were one of a kind
Specifically designed
To blow my mind
In a multitude of ways
But I lost sight of you

As I pursued personal glory
I thought you would
Wait for me
Fate had different plans...
But I was destined to love you
I'd be damned if I lost
Your hand
In the grand scheme

Pieces From A Beating Heart

You're all that mattered

The woman with whom
I wanted to start a family
The Queen I wanted to keep happy
Loving you made me King.

I'd stop at nothing
To see that smile
Even if it meant I
Had to make sacrifices
Like my arrogant pride
I learned that
When the love is real
You'll compromise

Not your integrity
But the energy
Necessary to keep
Each other happy
Fuck the world
Girl
You Are All I Want.

"Solo Cents"

Honest & Loyal
Your Love Is The Truth

Being real with someone isn't always as easy as we would like, especially when you care about them. However, there are long-term repercussions for lying. Even when it's ugly, honesty is always appreciated and respected, even if it's not initially received that way.

"Deeper PENetration"

She said,
"You got more game
Boy
Than a handheld."
I told her
I wasn't playing
Then showed Her
How a Man felt
The Attraction Made Her Wet
But The Connection Made Her
Heart Melt

"Solo Cents"

Home is where the heart is
Wherever you are is where I live

Absence makes the heart grow fonder. If you and your partner have to spend time away from one another, it should not be the end of your relationship or the beginning of insecurities. It's really an opportunity to develop a connection that transcends being in the same room. I'm not saying it's not difficult, but distance won't destroy a relationship founded on trust and communication.

"Perseverance"

We worked hard to build
What seemed easy
As natural as our connection was
Time had a way of changing things
We needed to evolve to keep up
We grew as individuals
To satisfy each other's needs
In our relationship
Mutually understanding
Communication was key
To the survival
Of what we built
It was not easy...
But you are worth working for.

"Life After Love: Part One"

He was telling her again how he would leave, but she already knew they were over. She was over the disrespect and the constant arguments. He was possessive and prideful, which often left her upset and confused. Who was he? The person he had become wasn't the man she began this relationship with.

He thought it was all good. He spoiled her with material things and considered that showing more than enough love. He believed he was in control of his emotions, that he had a hold on their relationship, and that she wasn't going anywhere. He acted like he didn't care because every time he became upset and left, she'd be the one apologizing, running back to him in tears. He'd even place the blame solely on her, almost as if she was the only one in the relationship.

She was sick of dealing with it. I was sick of hearing about him. She confided in me and I feared she'd never find the strength to pursue her own happiness. She was stuck in a cycle that abused her psyche and left her feeling depressed.

Pieces From A Beating Heart

I couldn't watch her go through it, knowing what she had been through, knowing her worth.

I sent her a text to let her know I was there. When I pulled up to the house, he was still acting tough. Suddenly, his bravado shifted to concern as she made her way out the door. He followed her outside as I exited the car to meet her. I grabbed the bags she carried, ready to bury her "boyfriend" if it came to that. Arrogantly, he asked me,

"Who are you?"

I stared at him for a moment before I began to respond, but she cut me off as she uttered,

"The man you should have been."

He stood there stunned as she got into the passenger side of my ride. He seemed like he wanted to say something else to me as I put her bags in the back, but he just walked inside. I expected him to fight, but his pride kept him from showing any concern over her.

I was hit with a mix of emotion as I got in the car and pulled off. Part of me was sad she even had to deal with that asshole. Another part of me was glad it was over. She needed the closure to move on, but I knew the process for her to heal would not be easy. Either way, I would be there for her.

She grabbed my hand as I drove down the street, but didn't say anything. I didn't know where I was supposed to take her, but I wasn't about to let her be alone. We had developed a connection and I couldn't let go.

"Are you hungry?"

I spoke as we pulled up to a red light, breaking an uneasy silence that had set in the car. I wanted to get her mind off of what just happened and provide a distraction that could make her smile.

She looked at me with sadness written in her eyes and tried to muster a response. She simply shuddered, unable to respond as tears streamed down her face. I pulled over and put the hazard lights on as she sobbed. I reached over to hold her and she collapsed in my embrace, her body shaking.

"It'll be ok," I comforted.

"I just," she began between cries, "I just wish he cared. He doesn't care. He used to care...Why doesn't he care?"

"I don't know," I responded, "I just know if you're not happy, you need to leave and find your happiness."

"I'm not happy," she repeated. "Why am I even crying?"

"Because it still sucks."

I heard her laugh as she sat up. A smile had made its way on her tear-stained face that seemed to brighten the car's interior.

"Ugh, You're so...," she began before stopping

again as if she had an epiphany. "I want to get drunk."

It was my turn to laugh at her change in mood and suggestion of plans. It was her night though. I was willing to do whatever it took to keep a smile on her face. I wanted her to know what it meant to be happy again. I wanted to give her that feeling.

"We can go somewhere laid back," I responded, considering her current emotional state. "I know a spot close to my apartment."

"You're trying to hide me huh," she responded jokingly, "I'm not cute enough to be out with you? Alright, let's go somewhere laid back...You'll see. Just drive."

"Oh," I commented as I pulled back onto the road, "Excuse me."

The bar I thought of wasn't too far from where we were. I tried to glance at her occasionally as she was doing something in the mirror. She would playfully push my head away if I looked in her direction. When we got the bar, I got out of the car to open her door.

From the moment she exited the car, I was in awe. She looked gorgeous in a pair of ripped jeans and a plain white shirt. I swore, I'd never seen a more beautiful woman. My eyes were drawn to the curves of her shape and the features of her face. Attracted was an understatement. I could not look away.

"You're beautiful," I stated blindly, to which she started smiling again.

"But we're keeping it low key," she responded playfully. "I hope you can keep up."

The drama from earlier in the evening seemed forgotten as soon as we exited the car. All my attention was on her as she walked and I wondered how that man could have lost sight of her beauty. The answer came to mind as we were inside the bar. Complacency was a common plague in relationships. People took each other for granted and managed to forget what brought them together in the first place. As we sat the bar, I thought, I wouldn't want to waste my chance.

I didn't speak a word of my thoughts. I wasn't about to share my fantasies with her nor would I allow them to dictate how I acted towards her. I wasn't trying to charm her or swoop in during her moments of vulnerability. My intentions were pure. I had her best interests at heart and wanted her to be happy.

We started with shots of tequila. I could still feel the liquor burning in my throat as she described the signs that told her to leave him. Like him being out and not responding to her texts. Like him getting upset because she thought it was inconsiderate when he was unresponsive. God forbid she didn't answer the phone when he called, all hell would break loose.

We took another shot of tequila as she poured her feelings out to me. She tolerated his attitude and ugly habits because she knew she wasn't perfect. She took blame for the way he treated her. Even when he cheated, she blamed herself. Maybe there was more she could have done to keep him from sleeping with other women.

I wasn't drunk enough for her logic to make sense. I couldn't understand how she could blame herself for the actions of a grown man. He wasn't a boy she raised, his behavior wasn't her responsibility. Yet, she took it on the chin and still tried to be better for him.

Tears were welling in her eyes as she told me her story and I admired her courage with every word. She spoke honestly about the hurt she endured and as the words flowed, I could see the pain go...She would glow with love again.

I wanted it to be for the right man. Hearing her story hurt me, made me embarrassed to be called a man. I mean, damn...This woman was everything most men could have wanted. Beautiful, smart, ambitious...But even she was treated like shit because her man took more interest in having sex with other women. It was a sickness, an epidemic that threatened to bring doom to mankind. Dramatic, yes, but I couldn't stress how valuable a woman like her was.

Our conversation flowed late into the night, past last call and after the bar closed. We sat in my car and talked as I sparked a blunt, which she hit once even though she wasn't a smoker. The weed was hitting, but I found myself getting high off her thoughts. The potency of our connection increased simply because we took the time to talk.

The sun was rising when we finally decided to call it a night. I let her know she could stay at my apartment and that I would crash on the couch, but she didn't want to impose. I suppose it was for the best as temptation threatened to break free of the boundaries I had set. Instead, I gave her a ride to her mother's house where she'd hide out until things blew over and she could decide her next move.

As I pulled up, I realized I didn't want her to get out, hopelessly wishing the night wouldn't end. But I had to play it cool. I was doing a good job until she said Goodbye.

Pieces From A Beating Heart

She reached in for a hug and her body felt good in my arms. Her head rested on my shoulder, and for that moment, I swore, I wouldn't let her go. In the next breath, she was looking into my eyes and I tried to resist, but I couldn't deny the passion I felt. Exuded in a kiss, the softness of her lips consumed my every thought until all I wanted was to feel them again.

That's what we did until she drew away, seeming afraid of what had just happened. I kissed her again, pulling her close to me so she could feel security within my arms. With my lips, I tried to show her that I meant no harm, that I considered her heart sacred, that if she happened to grant me her love, I would respect it and cherish her until our time was done. Reality hit as I remembered how fresh her break up was, knowing that perhaps I should have been more cautious.

The kiss became awkward and ended. She sat with me for a moment longer, pondering the space we had just entered, somewhere between feeling each other and friendship. Somewhere

between maybe we should chill and eh, just go with it. She shook her head and smiled.
"What a crazy day," she commented. "Call me tomorrow."

"Of course."

She gave me another kiss on the cheek as she exited the car. I watched her as she walked up the front steps towards her mother's house and waited until I was sure she was inside. Even then, I stayed for a moment, replaying the night's events over in my mind that seemed surreal. I tried not to get my hopes up, convincing myself what had happened was created by circumstances and the feelings I felt for her were momentary.

That's what I thought as I laid down early that morning. When I awoke that afternoon, things had not changed. She was still on my brain and I could hardly contain my joy when I noticed a message from her. A simple, "Hey", yet the fact that she had reached out opened a world of possibilities for me. Was I on her mind too? Was she feeling me the way I was feeling her?

Pieces From A Beating Heart

The questions swirled in my head, but I kept them to myself. I didn't want to come on too strong and scare her off, especially since I knew her heart needed time to heal. I was anxious to give her a reason to move past the pain, but I played my position. I handled the friend zone well because I really wanted her to be better. I wanted her to be happy, even if she chose to be with someone else when all was said and done.

We spent the day texting, getting to know each other with an enthusiasm reserved for those who just discovered an attraction. The physical aspect was there, but I was eager to learn what made her tick. I wanted to know more than what was on her mind.   I wanted to be intimately connected to her subconscious. I wanted her world to revolve around me because she was easily the brightest star I had ever come across.

That's what I thought as we video chatted that night. Every time she smiled, I felt a warmth wash over me that could not be described. It must have been my pride growing, knowing that she smiled because of me, knowing that I was making her happy. The feeling could not be contained and a smile would make its way across my face too. I couldn't help but notice how *her* happiness had such an impact on my own.

I reminded myself to slow down. I just didn't know how. My feelings were slowly escaping my control. The days passed, the laughs remained, and our connection continued to blossom. I was lost in the awesome environment her presence invoked and became addicted. I wanted to spend all my time with her. I wanted her to know the materials possessions of the world paled in comparison to the beauty of her person. I had placed her on a pedestal and she was primed to be my Queen. There was just one thing...Her past.

It held me back from fully opening up to her. As we grew closer, my need for closure became stronger. She mentioned his name less as the days became weeks, but I knew it couldn't have been so easy. History wasn't so easy to erase, especially when there was love involved. I trusted her word as she eased my worries, trying her best to make sure I felt comfortable. Insecure? No, but I needed assurances that she was committed to moving forward with me. I needed to know she wasn't looking back at him.

My need hit its peak one evening as I had gone out with friends to celebrate a birthday. She couldn't attend because of work commitments. We exchanged messages early in the evening, but then communication stopped. I let it slide for awhile, but I couldn't resist checking on her. I called and the phone went to voicemail. Something must have been wrong, I thought as I called again. She should've answered me.

When she didn't, paranoia took over and I began to think the worst. Maybe I *was* insecure. My blood boiled with a foreign feeling I could only assume was jealousy. Negative thoughts ran through my head. I concluded she had to be cheating. He had weaseled his way back in, but I wasn't about to lose her.

I had convinced myself of the worst and was ready to confront the situation. I left my friend's party and drove to her house, prepared to curse her out and whoop his ass the way I should have the first time. Her car was in the driveway and there were no lights on in her house. I knew she was trying to keep a secret, but I was prepared to make a discovery.

I rang the door bell and started banging on the door. Belligerent as all hell. At 2 in the morning. On a Thursday, as if tomorrow wasn't a work day. Obviously, I gave no fucks and kept knocking until she opened up. There she stood, in pajamas and a tank top with her hair wrapped, rubbing her eyes. She looked like she had just woken up, but I wasn't convinced.

"What are you doing," I asked menacingly, "I called and you didn't answer me."

"I fell asleep," she responded slowly as if it wasn't already obvious, "I got off work late and was exhausted. What's wrong?"

The look in her eyes made me feel stupid. I knew in that moment that I had jumped to a foolish conclusion. "Nothing," I began, "I was just worried."

"Worried about what?"

Her tone raised as she became more aware of the reality in the situation. My excuse wasn't going to fly and I wasn't good at hiding how I felt, right or wrong.

"I was worried...That you were with him," I confessed. "I knew it didn't make sense, but when you didn't answer my call, that's where my mind went and this is where I ended up. I thought you were with...-"

She cut me off with a wave of her hand as a look of disgust crossed her face. "You thought I was with him? You don't think I had enough of that shit? When was the last time I even mentioned him?"

Her arms folded across her chest and I tried to lean in to give her a hug, but she pushed me back and shook her head.

Pieces From A Beating Heart

"Nah, this is fucked up," she continued, "Why would I do you like that?"

Making myself look like a dumb ass was a sobering experience. I shook my head and continued to speak my mind.

"I fucked up and I'm sorry. I got nervous and over reacted...I just know you're not the one to lose and I'm willing to do whatever it takes to keep you. Even if it means driving to your house at 2 in the morning to see what you're doing."

She laughed at my last sentence and patted me on the arm. "Not him ever again, that's for sure. You're crazy, you know that?"

"Crazy about you? Yes, I agree."
She smiled as she took my hand, bringing me inside of the house and closing the door behind us. "What am I going to do with you?"

She was leading me up the steps, but I pulled her back into my arms. "You're going to love me."

Pieces From A Beating Heart

Her body felt so good against mine that we almost didn't make it up the stairs. I faintly heard her whisper,

"What if I already do?"

My heart jumped as I wondered if I heard her correctly. She turned around to face me and simply nodded her head.

"Stop worrying," she soothed, stealing my soul as she looked into my eyes, "I love you."

Pieces From A Beating Heart

"Bondage"

I tried to hold her down
Instead
I held her back
She wanted to be free
But with me?
She felt trapped.

"Alone"

Blissfully ignorant. My love could be next to me, but I was controlled by my lusts. Expressing that I was horny was more important than getting to know her. Knowing her body was more important that knowing her know a person. At the time, all I wanted to know was how she looked with her clothes off and if I could make her toes curl. All the while, my love was lost in the world, trying to find me while I figured, I was better off alone.

"Asylum"

Locked away in a cell
I scribble your name
On the wall
Key to my
Sanity
Without you
I go drifting
Into a dark asylum
Where Silence Deafens
And My Heartbeat's Missing
LISTEN
I Need You.

"Winter"

I usually hated the sight of her tears, but tonight, I despised them. She stood in front of me, crying uncontrollably, with her shoulders heaving up and down through each sobbing breath. She was trying so hard to hold things together while she fell apart. My heart wanted to console her, but I could not.

I thought about the times when we were inseparable. When her smile was my sun and being with her meant the world to me. My girl. It was a title I felt honored to give her because of how hard I had to work for her. She earned it and without a shade of grey, we were committed.

All in, at first. Perfect until we became comfortable...Until I became comfortable actually. I felt the pressure of being a good man some nights and folded, conceding defeat. Started spending nights away, started arguments over pettiness, forgetting how she had been there for me before we even made our relationship official. She could no longer trust me and those insecurities were a lot to overcome.

Pieces From A Beating Heart

She stood there crying, trying to explain what I already knew. One look in her eyes and I knew what she was about to say. She had cheated, I even knew why. I had mistreated her. Her love combined with how I acted drove her to hate me and the mistake she made was a direct result of my actions. I created the chance for another man to be with her. She wanted to stay together, but I knew her trust was just as fragile as my pride. Once damaged, things could never be the same between us. I did what I thought was best at the time. I walked away.

"Solo Cents"

He loved the idea
Of having you
But wasn't man enough
To handle the reality

Sometimes, we think we are prepared to handle certain situations until they actually arise. Relationships are no different. It's vital for us to realize when we're not ready to be with someone else so we don't continue a cycle of hurt. There's nothing wrong with taking time to heal.

"Solitude"

When I'm alone
I miss what we were
And wonder where you are
All the while cursing myself
For still thinking about you

"Faded"

She appeared classy
I brought her champagne
Only took a few glasses
For the facade to fade
Replaced by the nature
She tried hard to restrain
Lost in her lusts
She needed no love
I thought she could be the one
She just wanted to fuck.

"Attractions"

She was attracted to bad boys. The 9-to-5 type of guy did not appeal to her. She needed an element of unpredictability. She didn't want an emotional man who was so in touch with his feelings, always asking her what she was feeling, always needing to be reassured of one thing or the next...No. If that was a good man? She wanted a bad boy.

She liked dudes with tattoos who were mildly disrespectful. She wanted one who handled business in the streets, one who handled her in the sheets, and didn't compromise anywhere in between. She wanted him with a beard, preferably, heavily influenced by the sounds of hip hop, so they could talk the night away about the state of the rap game. She wanted a bad boy.

She didn't need to be told she was loved every second. She wanted to feel it. The excitement, the sense of security mixed with the fear of running those streets was an aphrodisiac in itself, to which she was addicted. She couldn't get enough of her bad boys.

Pieces From A Beating Heart

Bad boys knew no love. They grew up in cold streets, where love was weakness and money was everything. Where bitches weren't shit and stable relationships didn't exist. She couldn't get enough of them, but whenever they had enough of her? On to another just like her until either they got rich with their schemes...Or were locked up for felonies. Sad cycle, so often repeated, but she couldn't see past her attraction to bad boys. It kept her from finding the right man.

"Cup of Tea"

Right after 6 in the evening, his stomach was doing flips due to his hunger. He assumed she was hungry too and asked her what she wanted. She responded,

"A lot more honestly. How about we start with some honesty, can you stop with the lies? How about coming home every night versus leaving me to wonder if you're even alive? How about the respect I deserve as your girl? You claim I'm your everything but you deal with so many sides! Matter of fact...I'm sick of your shit. I want to leave. Good bye."

"Gone"

There was no cure for lost time. Try as he may, he couldn't make up for the moments he had missed. No way to erase the pain his absence caused, no way to remove the scar his departure left on her heart. But he could try to mend, staring with three simple words spoken straight from his heart.

"I missed you."

Those words reminded her of those sleepless nights. So many nights when she had cried, wondering why he had to leave, wondering what she had done. Wondering why she had been hit with that cliché line about how he "needed time." Time to find himself somehow translated into him letting her go to be on her own. Wasn't she worth trying to work it out, not walking out on?

He had returned home like a dog with a bone. Ready to step up and become a pedigree. He was ready to be the man she needed...All she wanted. He had roamed the Earth and confirmed the suspicion he had left with. There was nothing for

Pieces From A Beating Heart

him better than her.

She heard his words. The few nights when she was afforded sleep, she dreamt of hearing them. Him walking through that door, saying those three words. But the reality of the moment didn't measure up to the dream. He had missed her alright. By the time he was man enough to say them, she had moved on.

"Solo Cents"

I Finally Identified
The Enemy
That Held Us Back All This Time
My Pride

We often use pride as an excuse to justify our stubbornness. Perhaps we should take more pride in being kind and open to communication. Stop being standoffish and start talking...It's the only way to solve problems, if a solution can be found.

"Fronting"

You see
I was hurting
But didn't want to
Admit it
Instead
I pretended like
Nothing was wrong
But the people
Around me suffered
Because of my front

You see
I was miserable
And didn't want
To be alone
But the person
I wanted to console me
Was the cause
Of my pain.

"Double Standards"

He wasn't always man enough
To own his actions
He acted immature
Out of boredom
Often finding entertainment in places
A committed man
Shouldn't have been
Caught dead in.

He was living
So he claimed
But would be livid
If she visited
Anywhere as devious
As the places
He frequented.
He was a man though
Somehow entitled to slide into
Whatever woman he chose
Regardless of relationship title

Those trivial relations
Didn't rival

Pieces From A Beating Heart

His true love...
Himself.

"Misconstrued"

I wanted to be understood. I wanted you to be able to see there were more sides to me than the things your friends told you. They spoiled your view of me with their perceptions and I was upset that you allowed them to develop your opinion.

They were bitter, telling you a man like me couldn't exist, telling you love was a myth because their belief in relationships had died. Their happiness had been destroyed by lies. By the smooth lines of men who would say anything to get between their thighs without having any intention of staying...They were trying to protect you.

Maybe I shouldn't have been so surprised. I could only imagine the amount of times men used the word love to abuse your trust. I wanted you to understand I was not them. If they were what we considered men? I was an alien. If they were from Mars? The planet I was born on must've been unidentified. I sympathized with Venus and knew the power my penis held, so I used it responsibly.

Pieces From A Beating Heart

I wanted you to understand. When I called you beautiful, it wasn't because I wanted to get into your pants. It wasn't because I wanted to be your man. I called you beautiful because it is what you are...But the scars on your heart turned you cold to the world. Your friends made you deaf to my words.

You didn't want to hear what I had to say.

"Suffering"

I had all sorts
Of wild thoughts
I wanted to punch glass
Or drive with reckless abandon
Anything to replace
The pain I felt inside
To say I was
In a dark place
Would downplay
The severity
Of my surroundings
Without you
Life felt like Hell

"Smile Of The Broken"

There's a reason
She keeps it all inside
The pain was hard to show
It had become easy to hide.

"Life After Love: Part Two"

Intercepted messages suggested she was up to something, but I didn't want to see it. I dreamt of our relationship feeling how it did in the beginning, before we set off on this path we couldn't quite recover from. Back when she would lay against my chest, her fingers running against my skin as she whispered three words I had longed to hear for years.

"I love you."

She said those words now and I thought about when I couldn't believe I was hearing them...When I couldn't believe she was with me, when those words brought me peace because we were together. Those three words made me smile like a child at Christmas who received more gifts than the ones he wanted. I flaunted her around town because she was anything but a secret, even though I had every intention of keeping her to myself.

I didn't even want to speak on what I saw.

Pieces From A Beating Heart

I wanted to forget, bury the image deep in my head and bring back the feelings I once had. Feelings now fleeting as a sudden coldness began to take over my emotions. I tried to act like nothing happened, thinking I could move past it because my pride told me I was a better man.

It didn't matter. The damage had been done. Her behavior didn't change, but my attitude decayed. My sweet words ceased as I thought of how often she spoke to him. The man she ran from...The woman who convinced me she was ready to move on still talked to her ex-boyfriend.

I thought it was a bad dream. Seeing his name and their conversation was just a nightmare that I would awake from...or forget happened. I somehow managed to persuade myself that I would no longer remember the betrayal and initial anger I felt. Right or wrong, I dealt with it on my own, never once confronting her about what I saw.

I shouldn't have looked at her phone.

Pieces From A Beating Heart

She just happened to be in the bathroom and it went off. Seeing his name triggered a curiosity that overpowered my respect for her privacy. Even after the messages I saw, I still felt like I was wrong for looking in the first place.

Was I dumb? Two weeks later, the numbness has resided slightly and I began wondering about the decision I made not to say anything. The more questions I had, the angrier I became because I didn't have the courage to ask.

"I love you."

I heard her and responded the same because I still did, but I was hurting. Pretending I was unaffected by a situation I thought of daily, driving myself crazy while she slept peacefully in my arms at night. What we had wasn't right, but I didn't want to lose her, so I suffered silently, trying to recover from a blow I was unsure of to begin with.

For the first time in my life, I began to think my kindness was a weakness. My mother had taught me that my compassion was a strength, that my ability to forgive and move past things was a gift that shouldn't be taken for granted. However, as I sat there damaged, reflecting on what had been done, I began to wonder if my mother knew what she was talking about.

I was tired of feeling walked over, tired of being the shoulder others cried on...Who was there for my tears? Who would hear my trials and tribulations? Who would inspire me and guide me through the dark times? I thought I had found a partner in this girl, but her attention seemed to be elsewhere.

I could no longer take the game we played and told her we needed to talk. Surprisingly, she agreed to the idea without hesitation. I suggested going out for dinner, but she said she would prefer to come to my place. Her accommodation was comforting, considering how nervous I was. What would I say?

I spent hours thinking, deciding on a course of action. My brain was exhausted with the schemes and plans I had devised, but when the doorbell rang, my heart raced. The words were lost as I walked to the door. Those elaborate plans became a mess in my head as I opened up and saw her.

"We need to talk."

She spoke with a somber expression on her face. She didn't even greet me, but the irony of her statement was intriguing. I nodded my head as confusion began to set in. Was this the twilight zone? *I did something wrong?*

She walked into my small apartment and sat down on the couch as I locked the door. To ease into the situation, I figured I would let her express her issues first. Whatever her beef was, it couldn't have been as severe as my problem.

"Do you want something to drink," I asked as I walked to the kitchen.

"No."

I poured some dark liquor into one of my cups and

took a sip. Before putting the bottle back, I took a shot. I needed the liquid courage to deal with this uncomfortable discussion. I emerged from the kitchen and sat next to her on the couch, ready to say what I had to, but I gave her the floor to speak.

"What's up babe?" I asked.

She didn't respond or look at me for awhile. I began to wonder if she even heard me and was ready to repeat myself. I put my hand on her face and turned her towards me to see tears streaming down her face.

"Baby," I began again, "What's wrong?"

I tried to pull her closer to me but she pushed away. She sobbed harder and I didn't have a clue as to what I should do. She didn't want my comfort and I didn't want to show it, but I was so prone to caring for her. I stood up and got a box of tissues for her, trying not to press her even though I wanted to know what was wrong.

"This is so hard for me," she whimpered through the tears, "But I have to tell you."

"You have to tell me what?"

She looked up at me with her bloodshot eyes and shook her head, as if unable to continue talking.

"Baby," I soothed, "I'm here for you. We'll be alright."

She shook her head again.

"That's the thing," she confessed, "We won't be."

"What?"

What she was saying wasn't make any sense to me.

"Why not?" I asked.

"Because I can't do this anymore..."

"Can't do what?"

Pieces From A Beating Heart

She sat there, staring at me like a hurt puppy. My confusion was growing uncomfortable and I felt myself becoming angry. Things were not registering to me like she was speaking in a code.

"Can't do what?" I repeated.

"I can't be with you anymore."

I had friends who were athletes who spoke of having the wind knocked out of them. I didn't understand what it meant, but nothing else could describe the sensation. It was like being punched in the chest, I couldn't catch my breath. What hit me? I sat back with my hand on my chest and looked into her eyes.

"Why?"

She handed me a tissue and I didn't even realize tears were falling from my eyes. I was numb, shell shocked by her declaration. Turmoil churned within me as I burned to know the truth.

"Because I can't-"

Pieces From A Beating Heart

She started sobbing and shaking her head again.

"You deserve better than me," she continued but I cut her off.

"This is bullshit. What is it?"

"I..."

"I still love him."

It was worse than I expected. Never in a million years could I have been prepared for that confession. Even though they exchanged messages, I didn't think it was this deep. What happened to me and her? It didn't register to me.

"What does that mean?"

I asked as if I didn't know as the cold set in. I wanted it to be said as plainly as possible, I needed that confirmation. She had plunged the knife in and twisted, piercing arteries to puncture my heart, but she didn't pull it out. She held it

Pieces From A Beating Heart

there with those tears falling from her eyes. Telling me hurt her, but I was the one who was dying.

"I'm leaving you because I want to try and be with him again and you deserve a chance to be happy."

I sat there frozen as she stood up.

"Good bye...I'm sorry. I should go."

With that she was gone. As was my love because the deed was done. That night, I thought my joy for life had died. I thought there would never be another time when I would find enough faith in another person to open up.

I laid in bed, trying not to think, wishing I didn't feel. I didn't want to wake up, but I couldn't even fall asleep.

Soon, the sun was rising and my life was set to continue. It was another day, but I felt the same as the night before. Numb to the world.

Work went by in a fog. People talked to me, but I wasn't sure if I responded. I left early and didn't really have a plan on returning. I had sick days I could use. I needed to be by myself. I couldn't deal with relationships.

I wanted to stop thinking of them altogether. The pain she put me through was a lot for me to handle and I couldn't manage it. I ran from it, into a cubby hole where the world couldn't find me. Somehow, that's where you did.

"Offset Dialect"

He couldn't understand
Why she couldn't get past it
Shit happens
People make mistakes
You move on
That's it

She couldn't understand
What he didn't get
She was HURT
When she needed him
He was out sleeping
With someone else
After she had been given his word
That he wouldn't do that to her.
How could she get over that

"No Service"

The phone calls stopped
The text messages slowed
I knew you were busy
But there was a distinct change
In how our energy flowed
You told me
I was bugging
That nothing was wrong
Only to later confess
I wasn't the one.

"Submission"

She lost hope for better
And settled
For the treatment
She received
From a man who said
He loved her
Even if his love
Hurt her
More often than
It Healed

"Cause"

There was no shame
In expressing my emotion.
The shame came
When I pretended I had none
I played it too cool
And lost you
Trying to please them
It didn't make any sense
Trying to gain the world
I lost the only person
Who mattered in it

"Error"

Something was wrong. You held on, hoping he would love you the way you knew you deserved. You hoped he would see you worth and fight to make it work, but all he had was slick words and relationships with other girls that made you feel insecure. You tried, but you weren't in a relationship by yourself, that shouldn't have been how it felt. Something was wrong, but you needed to realize, it wasn't your fault.

"Gemstones"

His crown had bigger stones
He came with more gold
All I had was my heart
And you wanted more
So I'm left here rambling
Scrambling to put the
Pieces Of My
Life Together
I Thought
We Were
Forever
Now
I'm Forgotten.

"Nights"

Forcing herself to eat
Laying awake in her sheets
Sleep never came
She knew life
Had to continue
But how long would
She feel this way?
Unable to enjoy life
Without him
Forced to replay
The times they
Were happy
Over and over
Just to get over
The torture
Losing him became.

"Appreciation"

I would say
I wish I never met you
But the pain you caused
Taught me
How strong I was
So thank you
Asshole.

"Switch Up"

Whenever our communication broke down, you never tried working with me to fix the issues. You blamed me. You didn't try to see my point of view or understand where I was coming from. When the going got tough, you got going and said I was stressing you out...What happened to being down for me?

"Despair"

She feared being alone
More than she feared being unhappy
An unfortunate circumstance
Due to a romance gone sour
That sapped her strength
And hope for better
She figured
All men were the same
Why leave?

Pieces From A Beating Heart

"Solo Cents"

Love yourself entirely before trying to find a better half.

Don't depend on another person for your happiness. They can contribute, but it really comes from within....As does love. Don't search for someone to fill voids you have in life. Find your peace before trying to find a person to "complete" you.

"Peril"

I didn't miss her
My soul craved her
That's how the situation
Became so dangerous
Her Love
Was The Only Thing
That Brought Me
Peace.

"Emotional"

He cried. He had gone through so much suffering in search of peace. He was also the cause of so much heartache for the sake of his solace. Every loss, every lie, every trial and tribulation sapped his strength. The countless dates, emotionless sex, sleepless nights...All drained his belief. He would never acquire the love he desired. No matter how bad he wanted to feel it, love never appeared. That's why he cried.

She came in his time of need.

"Deeper PENetration #2"

I didn't ask,
When was the last time
You had sex?

I didn't ask
Who was the last person
You fucked?

I dug deeper
And asked
"Have you ever made love?"

"For Self"

Learned how to love life
Without having a love-life
Learned how to love me right
Then the right one came
Loving me the same way
She loved herself
Selflessly
We became One

"POW"

One day you were all in
The next day
You're nowhere to be found
I was trying to figure out
How you could say
No one was there for you
When you never
Stuck around to find out
Either way
My heart
Wasn't about to be
A casualty to your inconsistency

"Guarded"

"You're so strong."

The mask she wore was convincing. She smiled in the times she wanted to cry, but she did a good job at hiding her emotions. She did not want to depend on a man and love was not a necessity. She wanted to be successful without having to sacrifice her dignity for getting ahead. She was strong, but whenever she was alone? She had thoughts of when he used to leave her knees weak.

She wouldn't speak about her ex or to him, regardless of how often she thought of him. As a proud woman, she would never admit it out loud. Her heart pounded in her chest at the mention of his commonly spoken name, subconsciously hoping it was him, feigning relief when it wasn't. She found herself getting wet at her desk as she reminisced of their sex, upset because he affected her, more so because she wanted more. Of him.

His affections, his attention, fuck her strength. She wanted him to be the shoulder she leaned on,

Pieces From A Beating Heart

her eye in the storm, her calm when it seemed like the world was falling apart. He was smart and gentle, aggressive yet sensual, the things a woman wanted but could not find. He had them, but she could not commit to the thought of needing him.

She was a strong woman, capable of loving herself better than any other could...She needed no love. So when he came along, he was something she couldn't trust. She loved to spend time with him, loved his lips, his touch...But her heart had been hardened, she couldn't see herself falling in love. So when the lust ran out? Their time was up. Leaving him empty handed, wondering what happened. She simply adorned the mask that became her identity...A lifelong consequence of once loving the wrong man.

"Solo Cents"

Before him, you made yourself smile. Don't allow someone else to steal your happiness. It comes from within.

Love yourself. Such a simple statement, but once we get into a relationship, some of us sacrifice that love to fall for someone else. Our happiness becomes contingent on our partner and if we happen to lose them, all feels lost...But that's not the truth. Truth is, love and happiness starts with you. Love yourself.

"Blessings"

Just Because He
Didn't Love You Right
Doesn't Mean You
Should Love Yourself Less
Lessons Are Taught
So Blessings Can
Be Appreciated
Have Faith

"Matchmaker"

I wanted that type of love
Where we found
New reasons
To say it daily
An innovative love
Where we created
New ways
To express our emotion
As if saying it
Wasn't enough
The type of love
When you did say it
The words would hit me
Like the first time
I heard it
Can you say it again?
That's the type of love
I want
The type of love
That never dies.

"Blunt"

I was cursing her curves
With this four letter word
Every time she walked past
That described exactly
What I wanted to
Do to her ass
"Fuck"

In the very next breath
I was swearing she was blessed
It had nothing to do with
The swell of her breast
Or my wild imagination
In regards to our sex

It had everything to do
With what I could sense
She was not easy
The challenge was more appealing

I started feeling myself
Probably more than usual

Pieces From A Beating Heart

Because of how badly
I wanted to feel her
But I wasn't the type to flirt

I didn't have game
I was the type to say
What I thought and hope
For the best

I thought of what I could
Say that wouldn't make
Me seem like a fool
I debated for awhile
Because the only words
That came to my mind
Seemed so Rude

"I
Just
Want
To
Fuck
You"

Pieces From A Beating Heart

"Caught Up"

Defenseless to the trap she laid, I was caught up in her gaze. Flames ablaze in her eyes, I wanted to extinguish the desire that burned within her. I wanted to trigger alarms in her body that would leave her sheets soaked and douse the passionate fire that threatened to consume us both. She peaked in several positions before pushing past her previous limits in pursuit of a deeper connection. She affected me in ways I could not understand, yet I was never blind to the truth. I would never be her man. Whenever I tried to walk away, the devil wanted another dance.

"Zoning"

I often felt cursed by my compassion. In a world gone cold, it was cool to not care and I was constantly ostracized for giving a damn. In my mind, we all had a part to play in our existence and we were all too ignorant to the importance of kindness and giving. The awareness alienated me, leaving even I to wonder some times...Why try?

I asked myself that question more than once as I feared I cared more for the livelihood of others than they did for themselves. It was disheartening, the feeling of fighting a losing battle without an ounce of support, but I continued to fight for those who didn't have a voice for themselves, for those who didn't use the voice they had, I fought for us. Not because I considered myself better, but because I recognized we were all the same

She saw things as I did. The world's pain was our pain. It was on us to make it a better place. We had the hearts to heal the world, regardless of how broken the spirits. She was empowering, providing the energy I believed I needed to

Pieces From A Beating Heart

continue on. A companion in compassion, ultimately uplifting, she provided words of encouragement to anyone who crossed her path. I considered her beautiful, the way she provided nourishment to my soul.

I wanted to be there for her the way she was there for them. I wanted to be her rock, the one she ran to whenever it stormed, the one who protected her, the man who shielded her from harm. I wanted to be her encouragement, her nourishment, good for her mind, body, and soul. I suppose, I figured I already was since we had grown so close and wanted to close the deal. How couldn't she feel what I felt?

It got to a point where I could no longer pretend. She was everything I wanted. I wanted to be more than her friend. We could save the world and teach them love together...I just wanted her to take my hand. I told her how I really felt, half worried she'd be upset because emotional vulnerability scared me. She did me one better and expressed herself.

Pieces From A Beating Heart

"You're really a nice guy and all, but I already have a man. I don't want to lose you...Can we remain friends?"

My feelings were hurt by such a classic curve. I appreciated her honesty, but honestly? I couldn't stand the Friendzone.

"Castle"

Her heart was hidden beneath the layers she developed to protect herself from dudes who weren't true with their intentions. They mentioned words like loyalty and honesty, but weren't about the application of the concepts. Instead, they used them to get women open, hoping it was what they wanted to hear, but not her...She wasn't easy to please and even harder to keep. To hold her attention required nothing short of a King.

"Solo Cents"

In A World
Of Attractions
Seek Connections
They Last
Longer.

What looks good isn't always good for you. The physical fades, but intellect and spirit grow with age. See past the skin and really get to know someone. I see your face...What's your soul look like?

"She"

I tremble
At the assembly
Of letters that
Spell her name.

Memories of ecstasy
Trigger in my brain
Whenever someone happens
To say it.

Addicted to my Heroine
Her saving grace
Flows through my veins
I wonder if I'm crazy

All I think about is her
A grown man
Writing her love letters
Hoping one day

She'll open up
To these expressions
And accept
All I have to Offer
Pieces From A Beating Heart

All Of Me, All The Time
In Every Way She Needs
Forever; So Simple
"Over It"

Can't sleep
Can't eat
I know
The Love Was Real
The pain
Is part
Of the process
There's growth
In how
We heal.

"Solo Cents"

Some people don't deserve an explanation when you walk away. Your absence says everything they need to hear.

You tried, you really did. You gave it all you had, including chances you didn't know you could give, including a forgiveness you didn't know existed...And they still shitted on you. You want them to do better and know that they're capable, but you can't do it for them. If it's killing you trying to get someone to understand you, perhaps leaving will provide them with the right motivation.

"Prioritize"

As selfish as it sounded
She had to focus
On herself
She kept trying
To find happiness
In other people
She finally realized
It had to come
From within her
Everyone wasn't meant
To understand her path
And some felt slighted
By her journey
But misery loved company
She learned to love being alone

"Percentage"

I fucked up. I wish there was another way to put it but I had no need for sugar coating. The blatant truth had to be told more than once for it to register with me. I fucked up, which seemed to be a common trend in my relationships. I broke another heart trying to understand my own.

There I sat, with my packed bag on a park bench, trying to comprehend why I had hurt another good woman. It was not intentional, but that did not excuse the fact that it happened. And for what? Because I wanted to be with the boys? Because I wanted to prove to them that I was still the man? What a job well done. It cost me my woman.

I gazed up at the summer sun but couldn't feel the rays. My world had become cold and gray as my mind mused over the pain. I seemed to be better at causing heartache than creating love. The thought left a foul taste in my mouth as I questioned, why was it so hard for me to be a good man?

Pieces From A Beating Heart

The blatant truth...I still wanted to be a boy. I was unwilling to accept all the responsibilities associated with being a good man in a relationship. Instead, I chose to follow the rules I could and make excuses for those I thought were too difficult.

 Though my lips spoke of devotion, my mind, body, and soul were committed on varying levels, none of which were ever complete. That's why my relationships never worked. They were giving me a hundred percent. I only reciprocated ninety-nine.

"Glance"

I knew she was bad for me
The moment I laid eyes
On her
I wanted to warn her
Let her know
Passion was etched
Into my soul
So if she wasn't
Looking for love?
She shouldn't stare
But her lust?
She could not control

"True Love"

It's OK. I know you gave it your best shot and you thought I'd be mad at you, but I can't be. Even if we didn't work, even if I'm disappointed, I can't be mad. We gave it all we had, I just wish we had more to give. I just wish I could feel your lips again, I just wish it was the same. But it's not and that's OK. I love you so much I'm willing to learn how to live without you.

"Solo Cents"

A Boy wants every girl in the world
A Man wants one woman to share the world with.

Maturity has nothing to do with age. When a boy matures, he learns that multiple women are actually a distraction, while one woman provides the stability necessary to build an empire. Understand, every Prince Charming doesn't have the heart to become a King.

"Beauty Queen"

He thought you were broken
There was beauty in your resilience
Brilliance in your ability
To bounce back from the pain
As much as he hurt you
The love in your heart
Would not change
You were Still A Queen.

"Single, Not Looking"

The search for what
She considered a suitable partner
Was past exhausting
It seemed impossible
Dating was a waste of time
As she was often introduced
To whom men believed
She wanted to see
Not who they really were

She was turned off
And stopped expending
Energy trying to find a man
She began
To focus on being
A better woman
Ironically
That's when the
Right man came

"Scale"

You worked hard
For her attention
Then forgot
What she was worth
Becoming too comfortable
Is a curse
And a good woman
Is someone
No man
Can afford to lose

"Honestly"

I couldn't deny the feelings I had for you. You were intelligent, funny, and sexy. Every man could see it and I know I was fortunate to have your attention. I didn't take it for granted and appreciated every second we spent getting to know each other. Of course, I had those moments when I thought about us having sex, but being in your company was more than enough for a good time.

I couldn't lie to you either. As much as I liked you, my heart was still hurting because of who I once loved. It wouldn't have been fair of me to pursue you any further. This was torture for me, needing this time to heal, feeling like I wasn't ready to accept your love, but I had to trust my instincts. I'd rather hurt your feelings now than break your heart later.

So please...Don't make the end of this any harder than it needs to be.

"Solo Cents"

Don't Hold Onto Unhealthy Relationships Because of Nostalgia.

Moving on is hard, but settling for less than your worth is worse. You don't want to look back wishing you had left sooner because the longer you wait, the harder it gets to break bad habits. So you have to make a choice....Is history with the wrong person more important than trying to find the right one?

-

"Devotion"

I walked through the broken hearts
Of those who loved you
Before me
Unafraid that I would
Share their fate
One look in your eyes
And I knew why so many
Tried.
They failed.
They came with their hearts
I devoted my soul.

"Solo Cents"

The right woman will challenge you to become a better man.

When she is worth it, she won't come easy, but you will undoubtedly know it's her. You'll put forth effort in areas that you never have previously in an attempt to please her because you know what she has to offer. More than her body, even deeper than her mind, her love is divine. Don't lose her.

"Life After Love Part Three"

My world once held a certain zest. I used to feel a passion that could only be described as a lust for life. When it rained even on the darkest of days, I would still find a way to give thanks for being alive.

This storm washed away all hope for better days. I no longer saw the sun rays. I no longer felt the light glow against my skin. Without so much as the flickering flame of a candle, I was left in darkness. She was gone. I was alone, left to these painful thoughts that promised to drive me insane.

I moved forward in a fog with no direction and no purpose. I merely existed, wishing I could find my way. I hoped the memories would fade, and I was willing to do anything to erase the impression she left.

That was how my depression started. It was where my addictions began. I tried running from a reality I wasn't ready to confront. I faced blunts and popped pills. I chased shots of liquor with bumps of cocaine to alleviate the pain. I didn't want to feel anymore.

Certain days, I didn't want to be here anymore. I'd wake up on the floor of my apartment in my own vomit. I'd commit to never drinking or touching the drugs again, only to end up in the same predicament a few days later. My life was fucked up, and so I got fucked up to make things feel right.

But they never really did. I just continued to spiral out of control. I dug a deeper hole that was sure to be my own grave. I wasn't afraid to die. After losing her, I felt like I already had. So much of my time had been wasted, so much time that couldn't be replaced. And what did I have to show for it? Nothing, but bittersweet memories.

I didn't want to think about her anymore. I started entertaining other women, knowing I wasn't ready for commitment. I was searching for a distraction. They were looking for a connection. I got what I wanted by pretending to be the man I once was.

I pretended to care. I pretended to listen, knowing my only intention was to sleep with them and leave them alone. The way she had left me. I had a vendetta to settle. These women became targets to even the score in my wicked game.

Once they opened up and trusted me enough to give me their bodies, the game was over. I wouldn't call or give them a reason as to why I had moved on. I would just find another to distract me from my pain. I would find another willing to play.

It was turning me into a monster. My conscience had grown silent and my soul no longer spoke. Ice pumped through my veins, and my brain stopped computing emotion. My own heartbeat became a stranger I no longer felt. I had become a different man.

I desperately wanted to move on and let it go, but after all the things we had been through? After giving her so much? Ending up with nothing changed me into this person I didn't want to be.

Pieces From A Beating Heart

I no longer cared. I was just here, doing what I had to do to get by. I gave up on trying to build a real relationship. I put up a wall that I wouldn't allow anyone to breach. I couldn't handle the disappointment. The sex wasn't helping anymore. The drugs didn't affect me the same. I was fed up with the cycle.

I was so tired of trying. I was tired of being me. Tired of feeling how I felt over a woman who was happy with someone else. I was tired of lying to myself, pretending that things were alright when they weren't. I was tired of hurting.

My trips to the local bar were frequent and that's where I saw you. A new victim, I thought, as I took another shot of Jack Daniels. But my intentions shifted when I looked into your eyes. Beautiful like a white-sanded beach, those eyes seemed deeper than the ocean. As my own eyes coasted along your horizon, I realized why I was so drawn to them.

The pain and heartbreak reflected in your eyes mirrored that of my soul. For a single moment, we were connected as you met my stare. You looked away and I immediately craved to look into your eyes again. I couldn't explain the feeling and it was uncomfortable. I looked away also.

I ordered another shot and threw it back before searching for you again. I certainly found you attractive, but what I had felt when I looked into your eyes scared me. Curiosity overpowered my fear. I was now intrigued.

 A few stools away, there you sat, alone. You seemed oblivious to the world around you as you fiddled with a cell phone atop the bar. I watched as a single teardrop fell from your eye, slowly trickling down your cheek. You wiped your face before the bartender came and gave him a smile as if everything was OK.

I empathized with your pain. There were glaring signs that I could not deny because of their familiarity. Maybe that's what brought me over to you. Having never exchanged a word, I somehow wanted you to feel OK, even if things would never be OK for myself.

Pieces From A Beating Heart

You looked up as I approached and shook your head.

"I'm not interested," you said as I sat down.

"Who said that I am?"

"Why else would you come over here then?"

"The TV where I was sitting wasn't showing the playoff game I wanted to see. This one is...Is that ok with you?"

"Whatever."

The bartender placed your martini on a coaster. You fumbled around in your bag to find your money, but I beat you to the punch.

"Ugh," you groaned. "I can pay for my own drinks. I'm not about to talk to you just because you paid for this. I told you, I'm not interested."

"Just because a person does something for

someone doesn't mean they want something in return."

You laughed.

"You're not a person."

"What? What am I then?"

"You're a *man*."

"What does that mean?"

"You're a shitty creature, not a person."

"Whoa whoa! You don't even know me. Someone must have hurt you pretty bad."

Your words had hit me pretty hard. My heart knew I had tried to be a good man before. Yet another part of me agreed with you because of the things I had been doing recently. I wasn't carrying myself as man. I was acting like an animal.

You nodded your head as if reading my thoughts. "But I know men. And all men ever do is hurt me. All you guys do is lie and cheat. And you make women feel like they aren't good enough when in reality most of you men aren't good enough for us."

I thought about my own situation and how things had played out. You weren't wrong for your assessment, but I felt wrongly judged for whatever you had been through. I also couldn't help but notice I had been doing the same thing to women for the last few months. It wasn't fair...To me, to them, to anyone.

"So then what type of man is good enough for you?"

You shook your head and took a sip. "I used to think I knew. I used to believe he was out there. Now, I feel like he's a myth. Good men don't exist."

"What's a good man?"

Pieces From A Beating Heart

You got quiet for a minute as you slipped deeper into thought. I ordered another shot before you started to speak again.

"You have a lot of questions. Are you writing a book?"

"No. I've just been dealing with some things over the last few months. I used to think I was a good man, but the girl I loved left me for her ex. Now I don't know anymore..." I paused. "I don't even know why I'm telling you this."

It was the first time I had said it out loud. Gripped with shame, I stood up to leave. You grabbed my arm.

"No, don't go."

I couldn't pull away. My mind told me to run, yet my heart compelled me to stay. I couldn't look at you and tried to buy time by ordering another shot at the bar. Obnoxious laughter drew my attention towards the corner of the bar, but I couldn't see who it came from. There was a girl

blocking my view, but she leaned forward and kissed the laughing man to quiet him. Cute, I thought, as she pulled away and he moved forward to whisper something into her ear. My blood boiled with anger once I saw his face. It was him, the reason my ex left me. I immediately wondered if she knew what he was doing then began questioning why I cared. I wanted to unleash the pain I had felt for months on his face and break as many bones possible. I used to dream of the beat down I would give him and now, I had the chance.
But your hand was around my wrist. "Just because she left doesn't mean you're a bad man." Your demeanor shifted. "It just means she wasn't the right woman for you."

I looked down at you as bitter tears welled up in my eyes. "She felt like the right one."

"Maybe she was right for the time. Just not for life. You never know."

I looked at him again as he cuddled up with this new girl. "I wish I did know."

Pieces From A Beating Heart

"Don't we all?"

A silence settled between us, two strangers seeking refuge in a bottle, both lost in our own thoughts.

"I really came over here because I saw you crying."

I could see the shock in your face. Your eyes opened wide as you covered your mouth. I couldn't help but smile. Something about your eyes made me forget that I was even mad.

"You saw that? Oh my God. And so you thought I was an easy target huh?"

I didn't know how to give an honest response, and you eased the tension with a laugh. "A joke. You don't seem to be like that. Not like I know, but you don't seem to be."

I could have lied, but I had already confided in you.

Pieces From A Beating Heart

"I have been, but this isn't me."

"Then who are you?"

The question stumped me. I had a response, but what I wanted to say wasn't true. Honestly, I was ashamed of the man I had become. I needed to change, but how?

I ordered another shot as you posed another question.

"Who do you want to be?"

This one was easier to answer.

"What is this? 1st grade career day? I want to be an astronaut."

You laughed.

"You're already an asshole. Why would you want to be anything else? And don't forget you came over here to talk to me."

Pieces From A Beating Heart

"Ouch...I was just a nice guy a second ago."

"You don't know who you are, so what do I know?"

I laughed and nodded.

"I guess you're right. Maybe I'm an asshole."

"It's ok," you comforted as you petted my hand. "I think I like assholes."

I shook my head. "That's not good, now is it?"

You moved your hand back to the martini and took another sip.

"I guess not. But you don't chose who you love."

Your words struck me, and they sparked a thought.

"We can choose who we date though."

"Oh, Romeo!"

I chuckled and shook my head.

"No, seriously. Maybe I'm drunk but it sort of makes sense now."

You leaned in curiously as I continued.

"You know assholes aren't good for you, but you're attracted to them. They hurt you, and then you wish you had dated someone else, only to end up dating another asshole. Right?"

You looked skeptical, but I knew I had your attention. "Maybe...so what?"

"So...I was dealing with a woman who loved the *'idea'* of a good man. But I should have been dating a woman who *appreciated* a good man. That's why I stopped being one. That's why I was hurt. I was trying to convince her I was what she wanted, and in some aspects, I was. But she still loved assholes."

Pieces From A Beating Heart

You sat there silently for a minute and I could tell you were thinking about my words. I remembered the asshole I had come to hate sitting at the bar. Fists clenched, I thought again about seizing the moment. But in the strangest of ways, my own words calmed me. For the first time in a long time, I felt a sense of closure.

"I need to get my shit together."

You downed the rest of the Martini as a smirk formed across my face.

"I do too... But this is a start."

I ordered another shot.

"It's a start," you repeated as you looked into my eyes. "Make it two."

Pieces From A Beating Heart